DON'T BE YOUR OWN BULLY

By Kerri Golding Oransky, LCSW

Illustrated by Jason Oransky

Copyright © 2015

For Jaden

"If you have good thoughts they will shine out of your face like sunbeams and you will always look lovely."

-Roald Dahl

ACKNOWLEDGEMENTS

Thank you to everyone who helped make this book possible. First and foremost, I'd like to thank the many clients (you know who you are) who gave me countless ideas, inspiration, critiques, and editorial advice. I hope this book has helped you as much as you all have helped this book! Special thanks to Jack and Rosie who helped me pull it all together and reminded me why this book is important.

Finally, I have endless gratitude for my amazing illustrator and husband, Jason, who brought these characters to life and made them better than I could have imagined. Thank you for sticking it out and working on the book when I know you would have rather been playing your guitar. Don't ever let Comparing Candace get to you because you are supremely talented! I love you and am so proud of our creation.

BULLIES ARE EVERYWHERE

AT SCHOOL...

ON THE SOCCER FIELD...

AND SOMETIMES EVEN AT HOME.

It's not just other kids that can be bullies. That's right! If you aren't careful you can be your own bully!

Sometimes you can be meaner to yourself than anyone, at school or on your soccer team, could ever be. You can beat yourself up for small things and make yourself feel terrible. How? Well, there are a whole host of bullies that live in each of our heads.

These bullies are self-esteem stealers.

They put you down and rob you of your self-esteem. Your self-esteem is how you feel about yourself. If you have good self-esteem, you like yourself and think you are good at a lot of things. The brain bullies can change that. They can make you feel bad about yourself.

DON'T BE YOUR OWN BULLY!!!

You can learn how to become a Bully-Busting Detective and stop these bullies from bugging you so much. Let's take a look at the usual suspects.

THE BRAIN

LABELING
LISA

MIND-READING
MAX

GENERALIZING
JOHN

JUDGE JOANNA

COMPARING
CANDACE

BULLIES

MAGNIFYING MASON

DISQUALIFYING DAN

FILTERING PHIL

FORTUNE-TELLING FIONA

LABELING LISA

Name: LABELING LISA

Method of Bullying:
Uses her label maker to put negative labels on everything you do

Last Known Whereabouts:
Tennis tournament after you lost your match

Her Offense:
Labeled you a loser

MAGNIFYING MASON

Name: MAGNIFYING MASON

Method of Bullying:
Uses his magnifying glass to make things seem bigger than they really are

Last Known Whereabouts:
When you were getting ready for school and you noticed a pimple on your nose

His Offense:
Focused in on it and suddenly it's all you could see

MIND-READING MAX

Name: MIND-READING MAX

Method of Bullying:
Makes you think that you can read minds

Last Seen:
When you heard two of your friends giggling as you walked by

His Offense:
Convinced you that their laughter meant they were talking about you behind your back

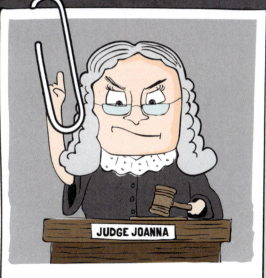

JUDGE JOANNA

Name: JUDGE JOANNA

Method of Bullying:
Tells you everything you do has to be perfect and that things "SHOULD" OR "HAVE" to be a certain way (even though there is no such thing as perfect)

Last Known Whereabouts:
On the soccer field after you missed a goal

Her Offense:
Kept pestering you, telling you that you should have made the goal

GENERALIZING JOHN

Name: GENERALIZING JOHN

Method of Bullying:
Makes you think that just because something happens once, it will always be the case by using words like "NEVER" and "ALWAYS" or "EVERYONE" and "NO ONE"

Last Known Whereabouts:
At school when one of your classmates teased you

His Offense:
Tells you "Nobody likes you" or "Everyone is mean to you"

COMPARING CANDACE

Name: COMPARING CANDACE

Method of Bullying:
Makes you feel like you are not good enough by constantly comparing what you do and how you look to others.

Last Seen:
In art class when you were working on your art project and peeked at your friend's project

Her Offense:
Made you feel like your friend's artwork was much better than yours

FILTERING PHIL

Name: FILTERING PHIL

Method of Bullying:
Filters out all the good stuff that happens and focuses only on the bad (his gold is the bad things that happen)

Last Known Whereabouts:
In English class after you gave your speech and forgot one line

His Offense:
Told you that you did awful on the whole speech even though you only messed up on one small part

***OFTEN SEEN WITH DISQUALIFYING DAN**

DISQUALIFYING DAN

Name: DISQUALIFYING DAN

Method of Bullying:
Throws out any positive feedback that you get, telling you it doesn't count (like a referee)

Last Known Whereabouts:
When you received the Most Improved Player Award at the basketball banquet

His Offense:
Told you that the coach only gave you the award because he felt bad for you, not because you earned it

FORTUNE-TELLING
FIONA

Name: FORTUNE-TELLING FIONA

Method of Bullying:
Makes you think that she can predict the future and tells you that things will turn out the worst way possible

Last Known Whereabouts:
When you were thinking about running for class president

Her Offense:
Told you that you were going to lose, convincing you to give up without even trying

Now that you know who the bullies are, you can learn how to stop them from bugging you and making you feel bad about yourself.

You will need to think like a police detective to get these bullies to stop.

There are several steps to thinking like a bully-busting detective.

STEP ONE: IDENTIFY THE BULLY

The next time you are feeling down on yourself, pay attention to the thoughts going on inside your head. This will help you figure out which bully is bugging you.

Are you saying something to yourself like:

"I SHOULD HAVE MADE STRAIGHT A's!"

That's probably Judge Joanna. She tells you that you should be perfect, even though there is no such thing as perfect.

Are you telling yourself you are not as good at something as someone else?

"SHE IS A BETTER ARTIST THAN I AM."

That's probably Comparing Candace. She will always make you feel that what you do is not good enough.

Now sometimes there will be an accomplice.

An accomplice is a person that helps someone else commit a crime. For example, if someone robs a bank and his friend drives the getaway car, the friend is known as the accomplice.

The Brain Bullies like to hang out together and often use accomplices, too.

For instance, if you are having trouble with your homework you may find yourself saying "I'm stupid!" or "I'll never get it right!".

This could be Labeling Lisa and Fortune-Telling Fiona working together to make you think that you will never figure it out.

Okay, Let's see if this is making sense!

Match the negative statement to the bully who said it. Remember, sometimes bullies have accomplices, so there may be more than one right answer.

NEGATIVE THOUGHT	BRAIN BULLY
1) "I'LL NEVER WIN!"	LABELING LISA 
2) "HE IS A BETTER SOCCER PLAYER THAN ME!"	 JUDGE JOANNA
3) "NO ONE LIKES ME!"	GENERALIZING JOHN
4) "I HAVE A PIMPLE. I'M UGLY!"	FORTUNE-TELLING FIONA
5) "I SHOULD HAVE DONE BETTER!"	COMPARING CANDACE 
	MAGNIFYING MASON

ANSWERS

1) "I'll never win!"–Fortune-Telling Fiona 2) "He is a better soccer player than me!"–Comparing Candace 3)"No one likes me!"–Generalizing John 4) "I have a pimple, I'm ugly!"–Magnifying Mason & Labeling Lisa 5) "I should have done better."–Judge Joanna

Nice job! Now, let's look at how to handle these Brain Bullies.

STEP TWO: IGNORE THEM OR TELL THEM TO GO AWAY

Think about how you were taught to handle bullies at school. The first thing your teachers or parents usually tell you to do is ignore that bully. This is also a good strategy to use with the bullies in your head. It's not always easy though. Sometimes these bullies will keep saying things over and over even if you try to tune them out. At first, ignoring them may not be enough.

You are going to have to get tougher with them and tell them to go away.

You can start by saying, "LEAVE ME ALONE!", or "CUT IT OUT!", whenever the bully starts talking to you.

Come up with your own words that you want to say to the bully and write them here.

THINGS TO SAY TO THE BRAIN BULLIES

1)

2)

3)

STEP THREE: LOOK FOR THE CLUES

Sometimes ignoring or talking back will work, but there are some bullies who are really stubborn and sneaky. They don't just leave. In fact, they will often keep egging you on and start making up lies to keep you feeling bad. This is when you need to examine the clues to see if the clues match the things that the bully is telling you.

Bullies have all sorts of tactics to make you feel bad. They tell you things that aren't true and things that don't make any sense. They can also be very convincing.

If you question what they are saying, like a detective, you can figure out if what they are saying is true.

Let's take a look at what happened with Sophia and Mind-Reading Max.

When Sophia was at recess, she walked by two girls and heard them giggling. The bully in her head told her, "They must be laughing at you. They are making fun of you. They don't like you." She walked away feeling sad and mad.

Now put on your detective hat and look at the clues.

Could there be any other explanations for them laughing?

Sure there could be!

Maybe one of the girls just told a joke. Maybe they were talking about a scene from a movie they had just watched. Their laughter might have had nothing to do with Sophia at all.

Let's assume that maybe they were laughing at Sophia. Examine futher to see where the laughter is coming from. Are the two girls Sophia's friends? If so, there is no reason to believe the laughter means they don't like her. Maybe they were just playfully teasing her.

STEP FOUR: TALK BACK TO THE BRAIN BULLIES

Now that you have learned to identify which Brain Bully might be bothering you, it's time to talk back to them with a more helpful and positive thought. Let's take a look at how to respond to each Brain Bully.

In the case of Sophia and Mind-Reading Max, she could tell him, "Stop trying to convince me that they don't like me just because they are laughing! I bet if I go over there and join the conversation, I will get a good laugh, too."

Now that you've seen Sophia put Mind-Reading Max in his place, let's take a look at how to handle the other Brain Bullies.

 ## Generalizing John:

When John starts talking in general terms like "No One" and "Everyone" or "Never" and "Always", look for exceptions to this. If John tells you, "Everyone is mean to you," ask yourself if that really is true. Usually there is at least one person, if not more, who doesn't join in on being mean. More than likely, its just a few kids who are being mean. Once you look at the evidence, you will probably find that to be true and you can tell John to take a hike!

 ## Comparing Candace:

When Candace tells you that your friend is a better artist than you, remember what Theodore Roosevelt once said, "Comparison is the thief of joy." You will always find someone who can do something better than you if you look hard enough. You will also find someone who can't do certain things as well as you. Your friend might be really good at drawing, maybe even better than you. On the flip side, there are probably plenty of things you can do better than her. Tell Candace that you are just going to focus on yourself and the things that you do well instead of looking at and comparing yourself to others.

Labeling Lisa

Don't let Lisa stick her labels on you. When she tries to call you a name, be kind to yourself and look for reasons that name doesn't apply to you.

 ## Magnifying Mason

Mason will use his magnifying glass to make things seem bigger than they actually are. When Magnifying Mason does this, ask yourself if it really is such a big deal, and if you actually need to be as upset as you are about this. Sometimes it's good to rate how big of a deal it is on a scale of one to ten, with one being not a big deal at all and ten being a really, really big deal. Then, rate your reaction and see if your reaction matches the situation (one being calm and ten being very sad, mad, or worried). If it's not a big deal (say just a three) but you are very upset (say a seven) then tell Mason to put away his magnifying glass so you can see the situation for what it really is.

 ## Disqualifying Dan

When Dan tries to disqualify something and say it didn't count, look for evidence that shows that it did count. If Dan makes you doubt why you won "Most Improved Player", look at all the positive changes you made during the season. Remind Dan of all those things and let him know that these are the reasons you earned the award.

Fortune-Telling Fiona

When Fortune-Telling Fiona tries to tell you she knows how things will turn out, tell her that no one can predict the future. Be like a detective and ask yourself, "What are the chances that this will happen?" and, "Is this what usually happens?".

Filtering Phil

When Phil filters out all the good stuff and tries to focus on the things that went wrong, do just the opposite. Focus instead on the things that went right.

Judge Joanna

When Judge Joanna tells you that things need to be perfect, tell her that there is no such thing as perfect. Remind her that it is okay to make mistakes. Tell her that everyone fails at things some of the time. Even Michael Jordan, the greatest basketball player of all-time, was cut from his high school basketball team.

Mind-Reading Max

When Max starts to make you worry that someone is thinking badly about you, be a detective and look for clues that support your worry. Then look for evidence that shows that this worry may not make sense. Ask yourself if there might be another explanation for what you are noticing.

Now that you know what to say to each bully, you will know what to do the next time that one of these bullies bothers you. Just follow the four Brain Bully-Busting steps.

BRAIN BULLY- BUSTING STEPS

STEP 1: Figure out which bully is bugging you.

STEP 2: Ignore them or tell them to go away.

STEP 3: Figure out the clues that support the bad thoughts and the clues that tell you those thoughts might not be true.

STEP 4: Talk back to the Brain Bully with a more helpful and positive thought.

Here are some Brain Bully-Busting worksheets to further help you follow the steps and ask the right questions.

Using the scenario of Sophia and Mind-Reading Max, put on your detective hat and fill out this worksheet. There are many correct ways to answer the questions and complete the exercise. One example is provided on the following page. Try not to peek until you finish on your own. You can ask an adult for help if you get stuck.

BRAIN BULLY-BUSTING WORKSHEET

What happened?

What was she feeling?

What is the negative thought?

Which Brain Bully could be making her think this?

Clues that the bad thought might be true:

Clues that the bad thought might not be true:

What are other possible explanations?

What to tell the bully:

(PRACTICE ANSWER GUIDE)
BRAIN BULLY-BUSTING WORKSHEET

What happened?
SOPHIA WAS AT RECESS AND HEARD TWO GIRLS GIGGLING.

What was she feeling?
SAD AND LEFT OUT

What is the negative thought?
THEY MUST BE MAKING FUN OF HER

Which Brain Bully could be making her think this?
MIND-READING MAX

Clues that the bad thought might be true:
THEY WERE LAUGHING AT SOMETHING WHEN SHE WALKED BY

Clues that the bad thought might not be true:
WE JUST HAD A SLEEP OVER AND HAD A REALLY GOOD TIME TOGETHER

What are other possible explanations?
MAYBE ONE OF THE GIRLS JUST TOLD A JOKE.

MAYBE THEY WERE TALKING ABOUT A MOVIE THEY JUST WATCHED.

What to tell the bully:
MIND-READING MAX...THERE IS NO GOOD REASON TO THINK THEY ARE MAKING FUN OF ME. THEY ARE MY FRIENDS AND WE USUALLY GET ALONG GREAT.

CONGRATULATIONS!

Now that you have learned the steps and completed the worksheet, you have officially earned your Bully-Busting Detective badge. This badge will help remind you that you have the tools to overcome those pesky brain bullies. You can use the blank worksheets on the following pages to help you bust any bullies that bug you down the road. Good Luck, Detective!

BRAIN BULLY-BUSTING WORKSHEET

What happened?

What were you feeling?

What is the negative thought?

Which Brain Bully could be making you think this?

Clues that the bad thought might be true:

Clues that the bad thought might not be true:

What are other possible explanations?

What to tell the bully:

BRAIN BULLY-BUSTING WORKSHEET

What happened?

What were you feeling?

What is the negative thought?

Which Brain Bully could be making you think this?

Clues that the bad thought might be true:

Clues that the bad thought might not be true:

What are other possible explanations?

What to tell the bully:

BRAIN BULLY-BUSTING WORKSHEET

What happened?

What were you feeling?

What is the negative thought?

Which Brain Bully could be making you think this?

Clues that the bad thought might be true:

Clues that the bad thought might not be true:

What are other possible explanations?

What to tell the bully:

BRAIN BULLY-BUSTING WORKSHEET

What happened?

What were you feeling?

What is the negative thought?

Which Brain Bully could be making you think this?

Clues that the bad thought might be true:

Clues that the bad thought might not be true:

What are other possible explanations?

What to tell the bully:

ABOUT THE AUTHOR AND ILLUSTRATOR

Kerri Golding Oransky is a Licensed Clinical Social Worker in private practice, specializing with children and adolecents. Jason Oransky is a graphic artist at the popular children's clothing company Carter's. This is their second book. They also collaborated on the book "How Zac Got His Z's: A Guide to Getting Rid of Nightmares." Kerri and Jason currently live in Atlanta, Georgia with their son Jaden.

Made in the USA
Monee, IL
06 March 2020